A story about awakening the

When the
Choir
Began to
Sing

Harry E. Eastridge, Ed.D.
William G. O'Callaghan, Jr.

The MASTER Teacher®

The MASTER Teacher, Inc.
Publisher
Leadership Lane
P.O. Box 1207
Manhattan, Kansas 66505-1207
Phone 800-669-9633 Fax 800-669-1132
www.masterteacher.com

ISBN 1-58992-118-6
First Printing 2002
Printed in the United States of America

A must-read for anyone who wants to make a difference

"*When the Choir Began to Sing* comes along when leaders need it the most."
— Richard O. Snider
Vice President, Barton Malow Company
Southfield, Michigan

"It provides a clear road map for working through troubled times."
— Gina Lucci-Spagnola
Owner, Dante Lucci Salon
Cleveland, Ohio

"This book exposes an important untapped source of power for leaders everywhere."
— Dr. James R. Rickabaugh
District Administrator, Whitefish Bay School District
Whitefish Bay, Wisconsin

"Reading this book will renew our faith that, despite the anger and distrust that currently exist in many parts of the world, most people care deeply and want to do what is right."
— Deacon Elliott Casalegno
Roman Catholic Archdiocese
Sydney, Australia

"The story which unfolds in this book reminds us that everyone has the power to make a difference."
— Larry Rhinehart
Human Resources Representative, Raytheon Corporation
Tucson, Arizona

Dedication

This book is for leaders and those
who want to realize their potential
to become leaders.

It contains guiding principles
and practical advice for leading
organizations and communities

beyond
the anger, cynicism, and distrust
that plague much of our society

to
a new state of mind
where growth and change are
solutions, rather than problems.

"The only thing necessary for the triumph of evil
is for good men to do nothing."

— Edmund Burke (1729-1797)

Contents

About the Authors

Harry E. Eastridge, Ed.D., has been superintendent of the Educational Service Center of Cuyahoga County (Cleveland, Ohio) since 1994. Prior to assuming that position, he served as superintendent of three Ohio school districts. He earned his doctorate from the University of Cincinnati and master's degrees from Wright State and Miami University. He is co-author of *The Power of Public Engagement: A Beacon of Hope for America's Schools*. In addition, he has written numerous articles, collaborated on a textbook focusing on the functions of a school superintendent, and consulted and spoken throughout the nation on various educational topics. He and his wife, Shirley, live in Sagamore Hills, Ohio.

William G. O'Callaghan, Jr., has served as a public affairs officer for a Fortune 500 company, written for a daily newspaper, and consulted in more than 150 public school districts. A recognized expert on the public engagement process, he is nationally on the cutting edge of strengthening the bond between educational leaders, their schools, and their communities. He is also founder of the Mohican Institute, a think tank for superintendents; editor of *The Power of Public Engagement: A Beacon of Hope for America's Schools*; and author of *Putting the Power of Public Engagement to Work for Your Schools and Community*. He graduated from Ohio University with bachelor's and master's degrees in journalism.

Acknowledgments

First and foremost, publication of this book serves as a fitting opportunity to recognize and thank our wives, Shirley Eastridge and Diane O'Callaghan, for reading the manuscript for this book and providing us with many constructive ideas for improving it. We deeply appreciate their love and support.

We are also eternally grateful to the following friends and colleagues who took their valuable time to review and critique the initial drafts of our manuscript. They are: John Barrett, Deacon of St. Peter's Catholic Church, Huron, Ohio; Dr. Greg Hinson, Superintendent of Fairless Local Schools, Navarre, Ohio; George "Hub" Marquis, President of Wallover Oil Company and member of the Board of Education of Medina City Schools, Medina, Ohio; Jennie Zamberlan, President and CEO of Avantia, Inc., Cleveland, Ohio; and the staff at The MASTER Teacher, Manhattan, Kansas.

Prologue

When the Choir Began to Sing is a familiar story about our on-going struggle with change. While this book is fictional, its story is currently being replayed each day in communities, businesses, schools, churches, and other organizations throughout our society.

While studying this book, the reader is encouraged to identify with similar characters and events within his or her organization and community. Such reflection can lead to a higher purpose and offer opportunities for people to interact with one another in meaningful ways.

Many of the answers to the issues and concerns that surface throughout the book can be found in the "Insights" at the end of each chapter. These insights lead to tenets and operational guidelines that will prove useful to those who wish to use this work to explore the importance of leadership and the pivotal role of leaders in an angry, cynical, and distrustful world.

The first insight is fundamental and relates directly to the title of the book. Specifically, how many times have we been told we shouldn't waste our time preaching to the choir—explaining our opinions to those individuals who we feel are already on our side and will support what we think and what we recommend when circumstances dictate a new direction? Composed of people of good will—whose hearts are in the right place—the "choir" can be a group of neighbors, employees of a company, staff of a school system, members of a civic organization, or citizens of a nation.

As a result of the widespread belief that we shouldn't waste our time preaching to the choir, the "choir" tends to be either taken for granted and ignored, or fed a constant diet of good news to keep it comfortable and happy. In both instances, the consequence is the same: the "choir" is put to sleep at a crucial juncture.

However, when preaching to the choir embodies urgency, motivation, and empowerment, it can inspire action in those people on whom leaders most rely. In this sense, not only is preaching to the choir a productive activity, it is essential if those in our society who believe in the importance of fostering the common good are to control their own destinies.

In addition to focusing on the importance of the "choir," *When the Choir Began to Sing* is a story about leadership. How do leaders make decisions? Where do they get their power? What do leaders expect from their followers? Who are the real leaders? How can they lead in this era of pent-up anger and growing cynicism and distrust? And how can they call upon the deep reservoir of trust and hope residing in all of us and inspire the small acts of heroism that make such a big difference?

This story is also about an organization facing change and the change. While the focus is upon the people who serve a church, it is really the story we all face. How can we deal with change in a constructive way? What brings us joy in doing what we do? How can we work with others who have different views? How can we participate fully while retaining what is important to us?

Coming to Midville

Frank looked into his rearview mirror and noted how a large patch of forest had been leveled to make way for more and more housing developments. On his right, he saw a winding, newly carved street with periodic signs indicating lots were for sale. The "Welcome to Midville" sign caught his eye, as did the entryways cut into a stand of trees to permit access of construction vehicles.

Frank looked forward to the meeting today where he would get to know his new co-workers. He had been hired by the Midville Chamber of Commerce and would be moving his family to this town in a few weeks. He glanced up and saw a weathered 4- by 8-foot sign proclaiming that Community Church, just four blocks ahead, was "Here to serve all and all are welcome."

He and his family had always been regular attendees of church wherever they lived. Oh, not every Sunday maybe, but regularly anyway. Frank enjoyed finding and investigating new congregations that he and his wife, Linda, would discuss. Is this the church for us? Could we serve here? Will it meet the needs of our family? Jeff, Frank's son, was now sixteen and would adapt to his new surroundings, just as he always had. Still, it was crucial for him to find positive role models who would also be attending Midville High.

Next, Frank came to the main street. It was still in a relatively small, central part of town. Some of the shops looked vacant, evidence of businesses that had opted for the new mall located just on the edge of Midville. However, there seemed to be continued support of the downtown district considering that most of the parking spaces were taken.

Frank nodded his head when Community Church appeared before him. It stood on the right-hand side of the street, occupying an entire corner. Fully-grown trees and shrubs that hugged the building, along with the discolored stones and rusty railing, indicated that it had been there a long time. Bright yellow marigolds drew Frank's eyes to the message sign standing beside the sidewalk. Yes, this looked like it might be a good church to pay a visit to.

Still having some time before his meeting at City Hall, Frank pulled up to the curb near a small grocery. The front seemed to be from a Norman Rockwell painting complete with worn bench, soft drink signs, and a bulletin board near the screen-door entrance. Frank entered the store and passed by a newsstand. He helped himself to a free copy of the local newspaper and then headed to the large cooler containing drinks. Cold air rushed out as he opened the door. He selected a bottle of water and turned back toward the checkout lane.

"The water's pretty good here, mister." A small, gray-haired woman greeted him at the register with a warm smile. "I know you can't always trust local water to be good, but ours is some of the best-tasting water around."

"Thanks for the tip," said Frank, "but I'm on the road for a while, and I plan to take the water with me."

"Well, I can give you some water if you have a container."

Frank smiled. "No, thanks. But maybe there *is* something you can do." He held out his hand and said, "My name's Frank. My family and I are going to be moving here and we'll be looking for a church. I passed Community Church just up the street. What can you tell me about it?"

The woman pumped his hand. "I'm Betty. As for the church, well, you see Community's my church, and I'd love to have you and your family attend, but things are up in the air right now. We have a minister who's been here only two years, and for some of us he still seems like a newcomer. Our retired minister was a wonderful man. He'd served Community for twenty-five years. But times have changed here in Midville. A lot of younger folks have moved out of downtown. You probably passed some of those new homes on the way in.

"Well, anyway, we've lost members, and there's some disagreement about whether our current minister really meets our needs. Everyone in town's talking about it, and there's even some talk about our choir. Can you believe that? Even the choir isn't good enough for some of our folks."

She paused and looked at the floor, then straightened up and cleared her throat. "The point is, we need more people with commitment, and I think we need to focus on what made Community Church a wonderful place for all of us. But I don't know how you do that these days. Our minister tries hard, but I'm not sure he understands our town or our church family. It seems like the loyalty so many of us had in the past is, just that, passed."

Frank could see tears welling up in her eyes. Yes, he would have to think about this and share what he had learned with Linda.

Insight 2: Even when change is positive, we need to grieve what was lost.

Tradition is more than history. It connects us as human beings. Whether it is saying goodbye to a popular community leader, tearing down an old building, or cutting down an avenue of fully grown trees along the main street of town, these are changes that disconnect us from our past and, as a result, from ourselves. With change comes a personal sense of loss. Even positive change can trigger deep feelings of loss. For example, in Midville, while the signs of progress were surfacing everywhere, the elderly woman in the store felt she was losing her small, rural community and church to a tidal wave of new residents. In this era of fast-paced change, we need to take the time to grieve what is lost, so we can move beyond the psychological and emotional pain caused by change and free ourselves to celebrate what is gained.

Wednesday Night at Community

Another Wednesday night and Mary was preparing for an evening like so many before. She bowed her head in silent prayer and anticipated what was to come. The choir would soon arrive and begin its weekly preparation for Sunday services.

Mary had been serving as the choir director for Community Church for the last three year since she, Bill, and the kids had moved from Springfield. Even as a child, Mary had been interested in music, and her work with the choir seemed to fill her with the joy of serving and knowing some wonderful people.

The door at the rear of the church creaked on its ancient hinges with the arrival of the choir members. A few members came in talking with their spouses, while larger groups hurried toward the coffee pot. Like every Wednesday night, the choir members looked forward to lifting their voices in song and enjoying the company of like-minded folks.

Friendly disorder seemed to reign, with choir members hugging one another and sharing the latest gossip, while Mary arranged her music for the final time. She said another small prayer under her breath, for understanding and a hope that things would work out.

Everyone was trying to be positive, but beneath the surface things weren't quite right. Dramatic changes occurring in Midville over the past several years were apparently coming to a head and fueling this uneasiness. Although it had been nearly five years now, many members of the congregation at Community Church were still very bitter about the closing of the old opera house in town. They also questioned the wisdom of the local board of education, which had recently tried to make major changes in the Midville schools. In both instances, the decision to make these important changes had come as a complete surprise to nearly everyone in town.

To complicate matters, Community Church was also facing a number of challenges. The budget was very lean and had been in that condition long before Mary arrived. Also, the congregation had decreased as newer church buildings had grown up in the fields on the sprawling outskirts of town. While the town founders had always supported the need for Community Church in principle, most of the new civic leaders had moved outside the town limits and found it more convenient to attend services in the newer churches. Moreover, several members of the congregation had not accepted the hiring of the new minister.

Rev. Kyle, the new minister, and his young family had adjusted nicely to their new home. For them, Midville seemed like a great place to build a future. In his position, he worked hard to meet the many expectations of his congregation. This was his first church appointment, and he wanted to do well. He had even had numerous conversations with Mary about the future of Community and how the church might better serve its members. Rev. Kyle worried that losing members to newer churches would weaken the church council's and the congregation's trust in his leadership ability.

The church council was primarily comprised of parishioners with family names long associated with Community. Their idea was to maintain the dignity of the church and retain things as they were, had been, and should be. However, there were some younger families, with growing children, now attending who offered much hope for the future and, while they were supportive, several had made substantial suggestions for improvements in the liturgy.

A number of parishioners had also registered their displeasure with various selections of music. Some members of both the congregation and the choir believed that the words in many of the pieces were so outdated they made the choral portion of the service irrelevant to current times. In addition, several new members questioned the capabilities of the choir. Mary did have to agree that she was short on both voice ranges and numbers, but most of the traditional songs of the church would have to be eliminated if this were the quality standard imposed. There was no doubt that the group had needs that were not being met. The accompanist, Jean, sometimes struggled with chords, and certainly there were members of the congregation who were more skilled and could have replaced several members of the choir.

The choir members were, by and large, lovely people, but the challenges were daunting. Most members were in the choir, not because they truly possessed exceptional voices or could read music, but because they wanted to serve in a way that made them feel an important part of Community. Contributing their voices was something they believed made a difference.

One such choir member was Charles. He had practically grown up in the church, and he and his wife had served on the committee that had hired Rev. Kyle. Charles was also a frequent contributor to the editorial page of the local paper. His brief messages addressed many issues facing Midville. Some members of the church and community viewed him as a voice of conscience.

Charles and his entire family rarely missed any service. There was only one problem with Charles's membership in the choir: Charles could not sing. As a matter of record, he was tone-deaf and would periodically be the subject of discussion when Clara, another choir member, would not only look exasperated at his attempts to sing, but would express very loudly that the group would sound much better if Charles limited his service to Community to areas not related to music. Charles was not the only member who seemed to have difficulty with the music, but his mistakes were the most evident.

Even Mary often felt the hours away from her two children on Wednesdays might be better spent in some other way. A new church had been completed six months ago only three blocks from her home, and Community was at least half an hour away no matter which route she drove. Her children had friends at the new church, and Bill had mentioned more than once that life would be easier if they became members of the newly forming congregation. After all, Community had seen better days, and Mary had "done her time." However, she also worried about whether anyone would pick up the mantel should she decide to leave. The purpose of service and the need to offer what she could was so much a part of Mary that she continued at Community.

With troubling thoughts swirling in her mind, Mary called for quiet and began practice. As she moved from side to side and heard the voices of the group rise and fall, she found herself looking more intently into the eyes and faces of those before her. Each member was here to serve, in his or her own way. Some were certainly more competent than others, some definitely possessed more skill than others, and some held a deep reserve of courage and commitment to stand before their friends and families and offer their voices in service.

> **Insight 3: Unresolved problems become unintended consequences.**
>
> *Unresolved problems trigger a stream of unintended negative consequences. For example, unrest over the demolition of an old, but treasured opera house had become a large magnet for negative thinking in Midville. At the root of this kind of unrest is the fact that changes in long-standing traditions are often made with little meaningful input from those affected by the change. As the resentment from being excluded from these important decisions grows, it forms a cloud of negative thoughts which hangs over an organization or community and serves as a dark lens for viewing all decisions. Employees and citizens then begin putting a negative spin on everything that happens, and the unintended consequences increase at a rapid rate. It is as if, one day, everyone starts getting up on the wrong side of the bed.*

Storm Clouds
of Change

The mower blades needed to be sharpened, but they would do for this cut. The weeds nearly outnumbered the grass, but Don fought the good fight and made the grounds, windows, and doors represent how he felt about his church. Fifteen years is a long time to be the volunteer custodian, but the work did not consume too much time. His regular job at the mill required hardly any overtime, so his weekends and most evenings were his own, or perhaps you could say they belonged to his service to Community.

Yes, it was a time to keep the old place looking good. Don had heard all sorts of talk about changes that were needed and how the church had passed its prime. He could not imagine going to another church, much less moving to another town. Midville had been home to him and his parents, and now he wanted his children to grow up knowing and believing in the same things he felt were so important.

Sometimes he enjoyed slipping into the rear pews of the church during the choir practice on Wednesday nights and humming along with the group. He knew almost all the words from memory, and it pleased him to see how the music director could lead the group, even if the choir sometimes struggled with the music. Mary had been able to retain most of her group even though the choir's best lead singer had begun attending South Church located just at the edge of town.

Don thought Mary was a good addition to the church. But, try as he might, he could not understand the irrelevant and petty bickering among some members of the congregation. And, no, the choir was not beyond some gossip and backbiting, nor was the rest of Midville. In fact, one of the church members who had left Community because of his discontent with the old ways was even spreading rumors about the new minister.

The former minister had married Don and Florence, and was the only spiritual advisor his kids had known until two years ago. But Don truly liked Rev. Kyle and viewed him as a hard worker with a great deal of potential.

Despite the gossip, things should have been going well. Almost everyone in town had jobs, and newcomers continued to describe Midville as the kind of town they had been looking for, for a long time. So Don couldn't understand what the problem was. But he wanted to help Community remain strong and sound for what he hoped would one day be the church family to his grandchildren.

It was Don's responsibility to update the church sign that stood close by the church entrance and faced Sycamore Street. He enjoyed the scriptural references and was pleased to note that anyone coming to town had a great view of the church and his sign. Each Wednesday he would collect the letters needed and meticulously replace the old message and change the dates.

Several folks knew that Don was responsible for the sign and had even remarked how they enjoyed the thought-provoking messages posted each week. But this Wednesday, the sign carried a different message. It stated that there was to be a "Special Meeting" tonight in order to determine the future of Community. He frowned as he moved the letters into place and wondered what other changes might be coming to Community and Midville.

> **Insight 4: Identifying the problem is half the battle.**
>
> *In situations where change is required, accurately identifying the root problem—or why the change is really needed—is vitally important because solving the wrong problem could make matters worse. In Midville, for example, the new minister may be the reason for Community's turmoil. If so, changing ministers may solve Community's dilemma. However, if he isn't causing the problem, replacing the minister may do nothing but anger those who want him to stay.*

Storm Clouds of Change

The
Announcement

It was only six-thirty, but lights were on in the church. Don suspected this meeting might last long after dark. The sanctuary had been cleaned and the doors and windows opened to allow the evening breeze to move throughout the building.

Members of the congregation began to enter, and as they did, they greeted one another warmly. Most spoke to Don and asked if he had any idea what was going to happen. The members had learned about the meeting in the church bulletin at the previous Sunday's service and were uneasy about the secretiveness.

Mary arrived at six forty-five. Following Sunday's service she had asked the minister what the purpose of the meeting was. His only response was that he needed to unburden some of his concerns to the congregation, and that difficult choices needed to be made that would impact everyone. Mary really wanted the meeting to end as quickly as possible. This was Wednesday night, and the choir needed practice in the worst way. She studied a new piece of music and wondered how the choir members would react to it.

Light entered the sanctuary in various tones of red and gold as more and more people gradually took seats around the room. The old clock near the town center bonged seven times just as Rev. Kyle opened the door to the left of the choir loft and approached the pulpit.

Looking out at the crowd, Rev. Kyle became aware of two things. First, the crowd was much smaller than he had hoped for and, second, most of the people in attendance were members of the choir. He cleared his throat and began a brief introduction of how he saw things changing at Community and what he was proposing as possible solutions.

"As you all know, we have lost many members during the last five years. There are numerous reasons, but the major loss can be attributed to our younger members attending churches on the outskirts of town. This seems natural since the churches are all new with great programs and buildings that emphasize more modern practices." His eyes scanned the faces of the families in attendance.

"Some of you have very definite ideas about what we should be doing differently at Community, while others want to retain the old ways. There is comfort here for many of us. The old doors were opened to many of your family members before I was even born. The old hymns have become part of our religious experience in ways not easily understood by outsiders." Heads nodded and everyone became more and more focused on his every word.

"As your pastor, I've attempted to listen to you and our church council in order to help me make this most difficult decision. Much prayer has gone into the decision. The council and I have decided that due to deterioration of the building, Community must be renovated from top to bottom. The doors and windows are in bad shape, the wiring is inadequate, and we need a new roof. In order to do this, it appears much more economical to either replace the entire building on its current location or move our church family to another location and build there."

Don was in shock. He could not believe what he had just heard. It was impossible to believe.

Mary looked quickly at the members of her choir. Everyone in the sanctuary started talking and asking questions at once. Was this the final decision? Where would they possibly move? Weren't there some options besides these? Why now? Perhaps there were other reasons why Community was losing members. Had anyone really investigated? How could the church leaders make such a decision without bringing this before the entire church?

Rev. Kyle answered a few questions about possible time lines, and several of the church leaders were the focus of attention as the meeting concluded. Most of the congregation shook their heads and spoke in low tones as they moved from the sanctuary to their parked vehicles. The minister said good night to the choir and departed, leaving Mary and her little group to close the building.

On the steps, in the parking lot, and along the sidewalk, small clusters of families gathered. Expressions of "I can't believe it!" and "This is the last straw!" were heard again and again. It seemed as if a close friend had been lost.

The sanctuary was abuzz with the choir members' concerns. Clara muttered, "Here we go again—they keep tearing things apart." Some nodded their heads in agreement, while others rolled their eyes. Clara moved to her self-appointed position at front and center of the choir. A community activist who seldom acted in the best interest of the community, Clara had a loyal following. She always spoke without rancor, but her words and actions skillfully exploited and mobilized the negative feelings of others when change seemed near. She knew she would be asked how she felt about these occurrences, and she needed some time to consider her strategy.

Charles stood for several minutes, listening to the various snatches of exasperation and confusion. "We just can't let things fall apart. There are so many good people who are and have been loyal to Community. I just can't imagine our wishes won't be considered," he said, though no one was listening.

Insight 5: People don't like being forced to change.

Most people are not opposed to change. Given enough time, they will work through the grieving process that accompanies it. However, most people are *opposed to having change imposed on them. In Midville, for example, the decision to build a new church was a top-down dictate that surprised and angered the congregation. People want to feel they have some control over their lives and they like to be consulted, especially about important decisions.*

The Turning Point

Practice was a shambles. Mary could barely keep her mind on the new music, and none of the members of the choir had any intention of continuing as usual.

Other than the choir, only Don remained at Community. He sat in the very back row as he had done so many times before. Don slowly lowered his head and pondered what Midville would be like without Community. He was startled to hear Mary raise her voice as she tried to bring the group together. "Listen, we can either continue our moaning, or we can prepare for Sunday. Which will it be?" The group clearly seemed bent on rehashing what they had just been witness to.

Charles was the first of the group to support Mary in her efforts to draw attention to the task at hand. "Why don't we *do* something instead of just griping about the situation?"

One woman spoke of her love for Community Church and how she would miss the unity. Charles interrupted again.

"Look, I feel the same way, but a poor-me attitude is not going to help anything. What can we contribute to our church family during these difficult days we are about to face?"

The group glanced at one another and then looked at Mary for an answer. From the rear of the church, Don spoke up. "Why don't you offer your voices to all of us in the congregation? We hear you each Sunday, trying your best to strengthen us and make us feel good. I think we need that kind of support, and I know the minister could use it. He must be feeling just awful about all of this."

Don pulled himself from his place and marched purposely down the center aisle. "You know what I'd like?" Without waiting for an answer, he continued, "I wish we could all sing together and see what Community really means, not just to me but for all of us who live in Midville. I certainly don't want to see bad things happen to our church, but maybe we can learn from this and grow together."

Charles moved next to Don and said, "Mary, we've talked a lot about how we need people to see the value of Community, and how we've felt under-appreciated, even when we're trying our best. I think we should examine our hearts and see how we can help ourselves face this uncertain time."

Mary leaned against the railing that separated the choir loft from the sanctuary and waited for other suggestions, all the time wondering where this might be leading.

Don looked from face to face. "What if we could capture our feelings of love and hope for our church? What if we worked together to make certain no one's left behind and that people really understand why we need to make some changes for the sake of Community's future? What if we could offer hope and encouragement to our minister, our congregation, and our town?"

Don had everyone's undivided attention. They had never heard him speak with such enthusiasm and commitment. It was as though something that had always been inside of him had awoken after Rev. Kyle's announcement.

"I think Don has something here," said Charles. "I'm certainly limited in music, but I bet if we put our best foot forward we could come up with a piece of music to represent our commitment and support for Community's past, present, and future.

"Mary, you've had more formal music training than most of us. Would you work with us to compose some music? This could be our way of helping."

Mary didn't want to tackle another job, but as she gazed from person to person in the choir and then from Charles to Don, she suddenly began to see how truly wonderful it might be to work on something so special and beautiful. "I think it's a great idea, but I will need all of your help, and this means more than just tonight. Are you willing to commit to this?" She heard a resounding yes from the entire group.

Insight 6: There is a leader within each of us waiting to make a difference.

In real life, leaders aren't always those who are elected or appointed to serve in formal leadership positions. Leaders come in all shapes and sizes, they show up at different times and in different places, and they are often hard to recognize. In Midville, Charles, Don, and other church members who had never before considered themselves to be leaders, rose to the occasion and began providing the guidance that was needed to save Community. By involving others in meeting the challenges facing organizations and communities today, we create multiple opportunities for awakening the leader who lives within each of us.

Creating the Music

This was it, the call to do something important and meaningful.

"Can we possibly get something together by Sunday?" asked Mary.

"I think it's not only possible, but essential that we're ready on Sunday," answered Charles. Don nodded his head vigorously in agreement.

"Look, I've had experience choosing words carefully for all those letters to the editor that I wrote. I think I could compose some lines that might be a starting point," said Charles.

"Well," declared Clara, "writing something for the paper is different from composing a song. I don't think it will work..."

Mary interrupted, "Listen, if you really want to take on this job, we have no time to argue, we only have time to get on with the business of pulling our thoughts and feelings together. We will need to put not only our minds but also our hearts into this.

That means we'll have to meet the next two nights. And I'll try to get my husband to watch the kids on Saturday, so forget what you had planned for Saturday afternoon. We will need to practice most of the day." She could see the idea of working through the rest of the week and giving up Saturday plans would require major rescheduling of personal calendars. Yet, one after another, as if on a mission, the choir members committed themselves to the task ahead.

"Rather than practice the music I brought, I think we should spend the rest of tonight working on the new song."

Several members gathered around Charles chattering excitedly about what must be included in the song to represent their feelings. Don walked over to Mary who was talking with Jean about the possibility of putting words and melody together. They were deciding on the form of the song, the time signature, and the number of verses. They were also hammering out details such as how many lines each verse would have and the number of measures in each line.

"I've always loved our music," he told Mary. "I can't read music, but I have some ideas how certain chords might really sound great coming from that old organ. Let me work with the folks who are putting the music together."

Mary smiled at Don. "Great! It'll truly be a miracle if all of this comes together."

The next two days were like a whirlwind. People throughout Midville could talk of little else than the possible loss of Community Church.

Friday night was going to be an exciting time. Charles almost ran down the aisle with his "poem," as he called it. The choir listened intently as he read the words he and his small group had composed. It was good. They had touched upon all the essential elements that made Community Church what it was.

One after another, the members turned to Mary for approval. She shook her head in amazement. "Charles, you and your group have done a wonderful job. Do any of you see some things we need to elaborate on or change?"

Except for a few minor errors in syntax or small breaks in the wording, the group was unanimous in its appreciation and support. Charles was elated by the group's reaction to the emotions his words conveyed. But he wondered if the music could match the feelings contained in the words.

Mary looked anxiously at the clock. Jean, Don, and their team were still not there. Fifteen minutes had passed after the agreed upon starting time, and everyone was conscious of the minutes slipping by. Suddenly the doors at the rear of the church were thrown open, and Jean, Don, and their group appeared.

"Sorry we're late," said Don, "but we've been at this all day. I had to take off work, and some of the others were coming and going throughout the day, but I think we have something."

"Well," said Clara, "the rest of us had work and plans, but we weren't late."

Ignoring Clara's negative comment, Mary looked at Don. "Let's hear what you have."

"We've had to improvise a little," explained Don, "but listen to the music and how it rises and seems to lift your spirit." Don nodded to Jean to begin playing. Some of the music sounded familiar as she started and stopped in an attempt to pull together the notes. But it sounded pretty good, and the melody was familiar enough that the choir would be able to meet the demands of the piece.

Charles, Don, and Jean then worked to make the lyrics and music come together. The rest of the choir huddled in groups and discussed what might happen on Sunday and how the members of the congregation might react.

Finally, Jean sounded a chord and the group quickly gathered. Charles and Don stood shoulder to shoulder as they carefully explained the various parts and words and how the music and lyrics fit. The choir listened in absolute silence as first the music played and then Don and Charles worked their way through the verses.

Even Clara had to admit, it was beginning to have meaning, and the lyrics and music did seem to complement each other.

Mary was ecstatic. She briefly wondered where all the talent had been hiding. It seemed as if the emergence of the leaders within Don and Charles had triggered a domino effect, as others in the choir began to take the lead. Worried the congregation and others in Midville wouldn't understand or feel the same way, she knew that she had to continue to serve with people like these. She could not bear to see her choir put so much into the song only to have it fall upon deaf ears.

Then the choir began to sing. Their copies of the words had been scratched on and erased, but their voices were clear. The music swelled from the organ, and Mary could barely contain herself for she knew they had done something few others would or could do. They had captured in words and melody the heart and soul of Community and described it for the world to hear.

Now they needed Saturday to put the finishing touches on the work and to practice. What a Sunday this was going to be!

Insight 7: Urgency focuses energy and drives change.

In crisis situations, a sense of urgency can clear away negative thinking that is rooted in the past and help individuals focus on what is important in the present. Most people are willing to support and even drive change once they clearly see the urgent need for it. In Midville, for example, the Community choir began to see things in a more positive light and worked to change the situation, once they realized what was truly at stake for the church.

Tears of Joy

Mary pulled the brush through her hair for the last time. Bill and the kids were waiting by the door as she grabbed her folder with the precious score, which the group had put the finishing touches on late the previous night. Mary's mind was racing as Bill drove the family to church. She was sure no recording company would offer a contract for the work, but it represented the heart and soul of Community and Midville.

The minister had readily agreed to extend the music portion of the service. The choir planned to sing the new song once and then invite the entire congregation to join in as they sang it the second time. Clara had typed the lyrics for the new song, and Don had made copies for the congregation.

Don was putting the copies of the lyrics in each of the pews when Mary and her family entered the church. Mary was certain she heard Don humming the melody while he completed his important task.

Promptly at eleven the service began. The crowd seemed to sense the importance of the day as the energy level in the church reached a fever pitch. Then, the choral portion began. Mary stepped up to the pulpit and asked the congregation to pick up the folded papers found at the ends of the pews. Looking from one to another, the choir readied themselves for what might be their greatest moment in the life of the church.

Mary instructed the congregation to read the words and listen with their hearts. Then she turned to the choir and smiled as widely as she could. With a wink at her group, she motioned for the accompanist to begin.

As the choir began to sing, members of the congregation as well as first-time visitors glanced at one another and smiled. They heard the true message. When the choir had finished, everyone stood and sang along. Many cried tears of joy.

The minister looked first at the choir and then at the sea of faces before him. The choir was doing its best to recreate feelings and thoughts about Community—all of which had been forgotten amid the cloud of pent-up anger, deep cynicism, and growing distrust that hovered over Community Church and the rest of Midville. He thought of the many times during the past two years he had spoken to the choir about commitment and service. The song was speaking in ways he couldn't. It spoke to the people he loved, and they appeared to understand.

> ### Insight 8: The "choir" is our connection to the rest of the world.
>
> *At Community, the choir consisted of a broad cross-section of people who had ties with other members of the church and with other residents in Midville. Since the "choir" knows or is perceived as knowing what is going on at all times—whether it be in a church, business, school, or other organization, it serves as a vital source of believable information for everyone else. For formal leaders and the institutions they lead, the "choir" is the link to the rest of the world. When the "choir" is ignored, it grows increasingly susceptible to counterproductive thinking and can become a negative link. However, when the "choir" is nurtured and empowered, it is a positive connection to others.*

The Awakening

The light on the roll-top desk lit up the legal pad that Rev. Kyle was using to outline his message for Thanksgiving Sunday. For years, preparing sermons for Thanksgiving and Christmas had been considered wonderful opportunities for ministers at Community to reinforce the importance of the church family. He wanted to use this opportunity to reinforce the work that so many had undertaken since that Wednesday night five months ago.

In the days following that eventful meeting and announcement, he had never felt so needed. He thought of the pride he had felt as he listened to the choir. Their simple message of hope refocused his energy and the energy of others. At his urging, candid discussions were held with all members of the church as everyone wrestled with the question of what would happen to Community. He also called on the church leaders to reexamine their positions and suggested that everyone needed to rethink where their decisions might take the church.

He removed his glasses and rubbed the bridge of his nose as he concluded the first part of his sermon. Staring at his reflection in the window of his study, he felt a sense of peace at the realization that he and his family had found a place where they were needed and where his congregation wanted his leadership. It suddenly became clear to him that the power of his leadership grew as he sought out the opinions and views of others.

Insight 9: The more power you give away, the more you get back.

In situations where a decision affecting others is made by only a few people, they often are powerless to enforce it as a result of the negative reactions of those not included in the decision-making process. However, when others are empowered to help make a decision, they will embrace it and support it. For example, when the minister of Community put a hold on the board's determination to build a new church and began engaging the thoughts and opinions of others, he was able to defuse the negative reaction and begin frank and open discussions based upon the facts at hand.

Reflections

Don and Charles moved through the buffet line to pick up their pancakes. The Saturday morning before Thanksgiving was the established date for Community to have its annual breakfast for the church family as the holiday season began.

Both men headed to a nearby table. They seated themselves so they would be able to see the children when they practiced their short program that was going to be presented at the Sunday service. Their talk soon turned to what had happened to Midville and especially to Community over the last five months.

"You know, I still can't understand why some folks don't appreciate the importance of Community in their lives and how crucial it is that we all have a part in making good things happen," said Charles.

Don took a long drink of coffee and set his cup down. "I've done a lot of thinking about what's been happening, and I know we've made real progress."

"What progress are you talking about?" Don and Charles turned to see Frank standing next to their table. "Have you guys got some room here?"

Charles and Don moved their chairs to offer more room for Frank. He pulled a chair to the table as Charles said, "We were talking about the changes that have been taking place here at the church and in Midville. Communication and understanding seem to be getting better all over town."

Frank cut a wedge of pancake and gave a brief wave to Mary as she moved a few of the younger children closer to the front of the group. "I think you're right. The Chamber of Commerce has been trying to get leaders together to talk about the future of our town, and they're asking anyone and everyone in town to join them.

"In fact, last Tuesday night, several of us identified over one hundred neighborhood and community leaders. We were each assigned to five of them, and now we're going to meet one-on-one and ask them what they feel needs to be done to turn things around in Midville."

Charles and Don paused to reflect on this news. Then Charles broke the silence. "When do you think we got it? I mean when did we start to turn so much of the negativity and complacency that was controlling the church and the town into positive action?"

Don looked down at his plate and then over at Charles. "I think it was when the choir decided to take action. Even Clara couldn't find fault with most of what we felt we had to do."

Frank studied the other two men. "I think the *lack* of action before that came from feeling helpless and ineffective."

Charles nodded. "During the last few months, people have begun to realize they can make a difference. Our church and the activity we've started is the talk of the town. I think the schools and the city council could learn something from our work. You just can't force public decisions on people. We all need time, and many of us are not exactly sure how we do feel about many issues."

They became silent as the first chords were played on the piano, and the children's choir started its program. After the musical presentation, most folks headed for shopping or home. Frank, Don, and Charles continued their discussion.

"I'm reminded of the company where I worked before coming here," said Frank. "We were facing some major decisions that could impact hundreds of families and the communities where they lived. The church council reminds me of how the president acted. He thought he knew what was best for our company. All sorts of money-saving schemes were put into place, and cutbacks were implemented in every department. We seemed to be fine in the short run, but when the economy dipped, sales fell off, and everything came apart. He didn't pull together representatives from different divisions of the organization to ask us about the various challenges facing the company. So, of course, departments began to separate themselves. No one felt they had a vested interest in the decisions being made. It was unbelievable. We had folks willing to help resolve issues, but it was as if no one could see or hear them."

"You have to wonder if things could've been different around here if we'd done a better job listening to people before the announcement about tearing down the church," said Charles.

"The opera house was torn down without so much as a second thought. Don, remember the problems we had in town when the school referendum was defeated? It seems like people are too willing to let bad things happen without doing anything."

Frank looked into his coffee cup. "I think that's common everywhere, especially these days. It's easier to point a finger at 'them,' whoever 'they' might be, as a way of explaining why something doesn't get done. It takes time and commitment, and that isn't always easy to get from people."

"You know," said Charles, "I think we could easily expand this discussion to improve Midville. I think Rev. Kyle would take the lead. He's really become a strong spokesman for these efforts. Besides the movers and shakers, we could also include the rest of the town. What if we scheduled forty or fifty neighborhood meetings in people's homes? It's a setting where folks will feel open and comfortable with one another."

Frank smiled and nodded. "Yeah, then we could bring everyone together and hold a communitywide meeting to make some decisions about the future of Midville. If we really work at it, I'll bet we could get four or five hundred residents to show up. In fact, the mayor, school superintendent, Chamber president, and church leaders could co-sign a letter of invitation and mail it to every citizen in Midville."

Don looked at the remaining parents as they gathered up children, while several others began to clean tables and carry the coffee pots into the kitchen. "I'm surprised by how fast we were able to get our people involved. I'm sure Rev. Kyle understands how crucial his support and guidance have been. And we already have the involvement of some key community leaders in this church—like you, Frank. You have a way of getting to the people who are the decision-makers, and then things happen."

Frank patted Don on the back. "Don't underestimate the leadership you and Charles and so many others have exhibited. You took a stand and acted at a time that was crucial. You weren't only willing, but you'd already proven your commitment through service. Appointed leaders can only lead when they understand what and where they need to lead the organization.

"I think of change as ripples on a pond after you toss in a stone," continued Frank. "Your influence moves outward from those most closely committed to the issue. As the ripple picks up momentum, you're able to bring more good people to support your cause because they understand how the change will make their lives better. But this requires people with good intentions to take risks and offer themselves to improve things for the right reasons."

Don pushed his chair away from the table and stood up. "There's so much to be done. Just here at Community we still need new doors and windows, and who knows when the furnace will stop working. I hope Rev. Kyle stays with us. He really tries to understand us. Clara keeps saying he should bring someone in to the church who could help him, but you know Clara."

Charles and Frank picked up their plates and followed Don in the direction of the trash can near the kitchen door. "I think Clara continues to focus on the hole and not the doughnut," said Frank. "That has been one of Midville's problems. There are so many good people here. I've found that you need to continually explore not only what someone thinks ought to be done, but also with what intentions."

Charles closed the lid to the trash can and turned to Don and Frank. "I'm not sure we—and I'm not just talking about Clara—are able to see the potential we have. That's what we were able to call upon. The decision by the church council to not proceed with its original plans but to encourage us to make our feelings known was a real turning point. That was a giant step. I think people know they have power, but somehow they have to find a way to use it."

Frank moved toward the coat rack and said, "Look guys, we've got some good things going, but they're only a start. The decision to restore the building, the efforts to attract new members, and our minister's constant reminders that we are an extended family—all of these things are necessary. But our challenge now is to keep our new 'song' real and the message relevant for everyone."

Charles and Frank pulled their coats from hangers and looked at Don. "Don, you've been pretty quiet. How do you see all of this?" asked Charles.

"I still think that we can't bury our heads in the sand. I want to see our plans become a reality, and that takes work. And speaking of work, I need to help the folks finish in the kitchen and make certain we're ready for our Thanksgiving message tomorrow." Don picked up the trash can. "Be careful. I heard that the weather may get nasty tonight."

Charles and Frank walked toward the parking lot and shook hands before heading to their cars. "Are you and Linda going away for Thanksgiving?" asked Charles as he inserted the key into his car door.

"No, we're staying here and celebrating our first Thanksgiving in Midville, and we're going to try to get a few things ready for Christmas. I'll see you tomorrow." Frank slid into his car and started the engine.

Insight 10: Preach to the choir...but in the right way.

In Midville, it was the choir that began to turn things around at Community Church. In life, it is also the "choir" of company employees, school staff, and community residents who have the power to rise up and make a difference. Unfortunately, we often either ignore the "choir" or we feed the "choir" a diet of information to keep it comfortable. In both instances, we put the "choir" to sleep. The lack of a clear sense of urgency and motivation also leaves our "choir" powerless. We must preach to the choir in the right way: wake it up and empower it.

Epilogue

Snow struck the window as Linda looked out at the trees and bushes at the rear of the house. She dried the last bowl and put it away. Frank and Jeff were talking excitedly about the upcoming basketball games. School seemed to be going well for Jeff, and Frank genuinely loved his work with the Chamber of Commerce.

"Honey, are you almost finished? We really need to get going if we're going to find a parking space near the doors. The lot's been all torn up, so we may have to find a spot on the street," Frank said as Jeff started for the hallway closet.

They drove along the same road that Frank had traveled months ago when he first visited town. As they approached Sycamore Street, Frank could see the outline of Community Church behind the large fir trees. Christmas—yes, it was that time again to share and celebrate those things that meant so much to their family. And here they were, readying themselves for a sermon and music that truly spoke to their hearts.

The church still needed new windows and doors, but they had begun to refurbish Community rather than tear it down or build anew. The emotional poison that had infected Community Church was losing its power and was being replaced by a growing spirit of renewed love, hope, and cooperation. What's more, there were encouraging signs that the positive, can-do attitude at Community was starting to spread throughout Midville. For example, a number of people who had participated in the rumor mill were now coming forward and admitting that they had been following the wrong path.

And all of this had been triggered by a few people who were inspired by a sense of urgency to write and sing a song.

Insight 11: When you are on the right path, you end up where you want to be.

Finding yourself on a path that is going in the wrong direction is a commonplace occurrence today. It is happening right now in communities, companies, schools, churches, and other organizations across our nation. Ending the painful journey down a wrong path usually requires a crisis like the "shocking announcement" about changes coming to Community Church. The sense of urgency created by a crisis such as this can awaken the leader who lives within each of us and inspire people to emerge and lead us down a different path to a place where we'd rather be. These acts of courage and leadership are occurring every day throughout our nation. Caring and responsible citizens like Don are showing up when they are needed to lead us on the right path.

There is a leader within each of us waiting to make a difference. Your time is now and this is the place.

Recommended Reading

To learn more about the thinking behind the 11 insights...

- The "choir" is an untapped source of power for leaders.
- Even when change is positive, we need to grieve what was lost.
- Unresolved problems become unintended consequences.
- Identifying the problem is half the battle.
- People don't like being forced to change.
- There is a leader within each of us waiting to make a difference.
- Urgency focuses energy and drives change.
- The "choir" is our connection to the rest of the world.
- The more power you give away, the more you get back.
- Preach to the choir...but in the right way.
- When you are on the right path, you end up where you want to be.

...you can read:

Bolman, L. G., & Deal, T. E. (1995). *Leading with Soul: An Uncommon Journey of Spirit.* San Francisco, CA: Jossey-Bass.

Covey, S. R. (1989). *The Seven Habits of Highly Effective People.* New York, NY: Summit Books.

DeBruyn, R. L. (1997). *Proactive Leadership in the 21st Century Classroom, School, and District.* Manhattan, KS: The MASTER Teacher, Inc.

Kotter, J. P. (1996). *Leading Change*. Boston, MA: Harvard
    Business School Press.

Lippman, W. (1922). *Public Opinion*. New York, NY: The Free
Press.

O'Callaghan, W. G. (1999). *The Power of Public Engagement: A
    Beacon of Hope for America's Schools*. Manhattan, KS:
    The MASTER Teacher, Inc.

O'Callaghan, W. G. (1999). *Putting the Power of Public
    Engagement to Work for Your Schools and Community*.
    Manhattan, KS: The MASTER Teacher, Inc.

Senge, P. M. (1990). *The Fifth Discipline: The Art and Practice of
    the Learning Organization*. New York, NY: Doubleday.

The Harwood Group. (1993). *Meaningful Chaos: How People
    Form Relationships with Public Concerns*. Dayton, OH:
    The Kettering Foundation.

Toffler, A. (1990). *Powershift: Knowledge, Wealth and Violence at
    the Edge of the 21st Century*. New York, NY: Bantam
    Books.

Wheatley, M. J. (1992). *Leadership and the New Science: Learning
    About Organization from an Orderly Universe*. San
    Francisco, CA: Berrett-Koehler.

Williamson, M. (1997). *The Healing of America*. New York,
    NY: Simon & Schuster.

Yankelovich, D. (1991). *Coming to Public Judgment: Making
    Democracy Work in a Complex World*. New York, NY:
    Syracuse University Press.